UNLEASH THE POWER OF CONNECTION

Stuck. Frustrated. Full of potential—but always falling short? It's not your fault. You were never meant to do this alone

DENNIS A. MCCURDY

Copyright 2024 - All rights reserved.

Unleash The Power Of Connection©
Dennis A. McCurdy, Adam Beck Publishing

Illustrations by Patrick Carlson

The content contained within this book may not be reproduced, duplicated, or transmitted without direct written permission from the author or the publisher.

Under no circumstances will any blame or legal responsibility be held against the publisher or author for any damages, reparation, or monetary loss due to the information contained within this book, either directly or indirectly.

Legal Notice: This book is copyright-protected and is only for personal use. You cannot amend, distribute, sell, use, quote, or paraphrase any part of its content without the author's or publisher's consent.

Disclaimer Notice: Please note that the information contained within this document is for educational and entertainment purposes only. All efforts have been made to present accurate, up-to-date, reliable, and complete information.

The publisher and author assume no responsibility for damages or losses resulting from the use of information in this book.

For more information: **mccurdydennis@gmail.com**

ISBN: 978-0-9798863-5-5

Contents

About the Author 1
Preface 3
Dedication 6

Chapter 1: Resolution Revolution: Making Changes That Stick... 7

Chapter 2: Who Am I Really? A Hilarious Journey to Self-Discovery 23

Chapter 3: Mission Impossible? Setting Goals I Might Actually Reach 35

Chapter 4: The Valley of Dead Dreams: When Goals Get Tangled in Reality 47

Chapter 5: From Idea to Action: How Mastermind Groups Dive Results 53

Chapter 6: Mastermind: The Secret Sauce for Success 65

Chapter 7: The Case for Collaboration: Why Mastermind Groups Matter 71

Chapter 8: Under the Spotlight: Thriving in the Presence of Accountability..................................... 81

Chapter 9: From Peer Support to Expert Guidance: Types of Mastermind Groups 89

Chapter 10: Annual Letter to Self 95

Chapter 11: Finding Your Pace and Your A Team: The Key to Sustainable Success 105

Chapter 12: The Power of Goal Buddies, Coaches, and Mentors: Your Shortcut to Success 109

Chapter 13: Finding Your Tribe: Selecting Members for Maximum Impact 119

Chapter 14: Meeting Structure Options 123

Chapter 15: Commitment Devices (Bonus Chapter) 129

Conclusion: Continue the Journey, Life Long Allies 141

Bulk Order Page 147

About the Author

Dennis A. McCurdy

Since the age of 23, Dennis has been a self-made businessman, building a reputation for understanding what it takes to succeed. He founded the McCurdy Group, which earned the prestigious 5-Star Designation in 2003, and has launched ten businesses, buying, owning, selling, and rehabilitating millions of dollars in real estate.

UNLEASH THE POWER OF CONNECTION

Dennis is also a sought-after speaker on personal development and growth. His five-week workshop, *Find A Way*, is designed for individuals ready to reignite their lives, chase their dreams, and discover new paths to achieve them.

Attendees consistently praise Dennis for his no-nonsense, practical approach—no fluff, just actionable insights.

He's the author of, *Find A Way: A Guide to Getting the Most from Life* and *52 Ways to Find A Way*, *Suck It Up, Cupcake: How to Stop Screwing Yourself and Get the Life You Want* and now *Unleash The Power Of Connection*.

Dennis grew up in a small, rural New England town without successful role models, so he speaks from the perspective of the average person striving for greatness. He's lived his message, not just talked about it. A USAF Security Forces war veteran, Dennis knows the value of resilience and determination and brings that wisdom to everything he does.

Preface

"We have an irresistible need to belong."

— Adam Smith

The original title of this book was *The Magic of Mastermind* because when you truly embrace the ideas and tools inside, it *feels* like magic. A mastermind group, goal buddy, accountability partner, mentor, or coach isn't just a nice-to-have; they're game-changers. Open yourself up to the process. Yes, it can be a little scary at first, and yes, it might be wildly exciting. Either way, if you lean in and give it a real shot, chances are you'll look back and feel nothing but gratitude.

A good mastermind group, a goal buddy, an accountability partner, a mentor, or a coach is magic.

You've tried everything, but you're still stuck. There could be several reasons, but the main reason is that you don't have accountability. In other words, you can lie to yourself and keep doing the same things over and over again, and there's no reason to stop because there is no one except you to hold you accountable.

UNLEASH THE POWER OF CONNECTION

No need to worry; you are no different from millions of others, and there is help.

Over the years, I have observed many things. One is that I do better on a team, in a group, or with a partner. The nudge I need pushes me forward, and I often need a push. Left to my own devices, I can become lazy, distracted, doubtful, and quickly attracted to the next new shiny thing. If you do the same, no worries; you are just human. The only beings with superhuman abilities are fictional characters found in movies. My most successful times were when I was part of the right group and received the right push. There is no doubt about it; we all need a push.

I believe in the power of connection and the strength of the group. I am not alone in this belief. Individuals such as Benjamin Franklin, Thomas Edison, and Andrew Carnegie understood the importance of connection and collaboration.

Mastermind groups and accountability partners are the magical tools that can take us where we want to go. Even if we don't know our destination, they can help us clarify our goals and find the path to success. The process works when you learn to listen, remain open, understand your limits and limitations, and, most importantly, recognize your potential and possibilities, moving past your biggest obstacle—YOURSELF.

Since you are reading this book, you're likely ready to elevate your game. Joining a mastermind group or finding an accountability partner, mentor, coach, or goal buddy will accelerate your progress.

No matter where you are—whether a beginner, entrepreneur, or executive—the key to your success lies in the profound

connections you cultivate. Harness and unleash the power of connection, embrace the support of your tribe, and witness the magic unfold in your life. Here's to your unwavering commitment and remarkable achievements. Let the journey to greatness begin!

Let's embark on a journey to discover how the power of connection can benefit you. By the way, you'll find that I'm very fond of quotes.

> *"For the strength of the Pack is the Wolf, and the strength of the Wolf is the Pack."*
>
> — Rudyard Kipling, The Jungle Book

Dedication

Like my others, writing this book has been an enriching journey. To those who supported me, you know who you are, and I'm genuinely grateful.

Most of all, this book is dedicated to *you,* an enriching reader who strives for more. More growth, more purpose, more joy. If you're someone who's ready to live better, dream bigger, and become the best version of yourself, then this book is for you.

Let's get started. Your next chapter begins now.

1

Resolution Revolution: Making Changes That Stick

DENNIS A. McCURDY

> *"One day, we will all be haunted by the ghosts of things never done, goals never achieved, and potential never developed."*
>
> — Dennis A. McCurdy

The road to hell is paved with good intentions

Before we go any further, I have something essential to share. You might not want to hear it, but it's the most reliable, no-BS secret out there:

Nothing changes until you decide to take action. Period. That's the end of the story.

You might think, *"Alright, I've heard that before. I get it."*

My question is, do you? Really? And more importantly, are you doing it *right now*?

Think about how often people—me, you, all of us—buy a book, maybe skim a few pages, and then... nothing. No action. Or worse—we don't even crack it open. Zero movement. Zero change.

You may have listened to YouTube videos or DVDs, attended seminars, and done nothing or given up after a short time. I am writing this book and keeping it brief so you will read it and learn about the Mastermind Group concept and how it builds accountability and cuts through the BS.

Most of us (perhaps even you) spend too much time BS-ing and making excuses. Oh, and don't get me wrong; this includes me too! Anyone who pretends to be perfect or has all the answers is full of crap. And as my friend Charlie likes to say, "Stop looking for excuses as if there is a reward."

So go ahead and make your day... and life. Take action!

New Year's Resolutions

The funny thing is that most of the things we resolve to do are good and will help us improve, make life better, and keep us healthy. Yet, how long do they usually last?

Academics have spent decades studying people who make New Year's resolutions. The consensus is that 8% of those who make New Year's resolutions do the work and complete them. This means 92% quit and make the same resolutions the following year.

Here are a few synonyms for the word resolution: intention, resolve, aim, commitment, pledge, goal, and promise. We are good at breaking all of those. And before you get down on yourself, understand that if you're doing this, you're human. Remember: Do not beat yourself up. If beating yourself up worked, you'd be perfect by now. That doesn't mean you shouldn't be honest with yourself or shy away from facing reality. It means being kind to yourself, working to improve the odds, building a strategy, and getting help. Finding or starting a Mastermind Group is a great start.

It Is About the Struggle, the Journey (Self-sabotage)

Did you ever see a professional athlete, actor, comedian, businessperson, writer, teacher, musician, or politician go off the deep end? Self-sabotage, acting out with sex, drugs, or rock and roll, gambling, bad investments, lying, tax evasion, or scandals? They had almost everything anyone could want. Why would they do this?

I've often thought about this. Success isn't the final destination; it is about the struggles and the journey, even though it can be difficult at times. People can go haywire when they win the big battle and hit the target. They lose their impetus, reasons, and need to struggle, which gives them energy, drive, and a reason to get up every day, even when it can be hard. If things become too easy, too relaxed, and there are no challenges, we can self-sabotage.

Human beings need something to look forward to, work toward, and keep us going. When we were primitive, it was all about survival—a never-ending, complex, and critical path to survival. We never lost that need to get up daily, hunt for food and shelter, and care for and protect our families from starvation and danger. It was a matter of life and death, literally.

One hundred years ago, the average person worked 2,600 hours per year. They didn't have time to worry about anything and didn't need to be distracted; they were too tired. Compare that to the 1,400 hours the average person works today, and they think they're overworked. Yet, they have no money, can't pay their bills, or save for retirement. Still, they drown themselves in their leisure time with video games, useless things, TV, alcohol, drugs, sports (watching, not playing), shopping, or whatever because they "deserve it." It's a bill of goods we have been sold to keep us stuck.

Avoid getting caught up in the Thick of Thin Things

The world is overflowing with distractions—more today than ever before. Not only are there endless temptations vying for our attention, but countless triggers pull us toward them. The media is a major culprit, social media adds fuel to the fire, and perhaps the greatest distraction of all sits right in our hands: our devices.

Cell phones and computers provide constant and easy access to distractions at any time and place. We are leaving little time for focus, deep thinking, and taking action, which hinders our ability to achieve our goals. It's tempting to distract yourself whenever you feel uncomfortable or bored by checking your feeds, playing games, or watching YouTube.

Like many other things, our devices can be a double-edged sword. They are great tools, but also terrible distractions. When used correctly, they help us create marvelous, productive, and fulfilling lives; However, when misused, they can lead us to waste time and become unproductive.

This is what I mean by "being caught up in the thick of thin things," which refers to engaging in activities with little meaning versus being productive. I understand it's hard to give up on our devices and the distractions they offer. As I once read, "We are drunk on our distractions." The Mastermind process will help you gain focus and reduce or overcome "*thin things*."

My First Encounter with Mastermind Groups and Accountability Partners

Marshall Goldsmith once said, "Control your environment, or your environment will control you." We often think of our environment as the physical spaces and objects around us; however, we must consider another significant element: the people we surround ourselves with. Our thoughts shape our limits and what we believe is possible, and the people we choose to be around directly influence how we think and perceive our limits and possibilities.

Bob Plourde

Bob Plourde was my first workout buddy. We grew up together in the small town of Brimfield, Massachusetts, just a mile and a half apart; we were the same age and attended the same school.

I acquired my first set of 110-pound barbells at the age of thirteen. They came with a bar, two dumbbells, and a Charles Atlas exercise routine chart. Bob and I made a makeshift bench press using a piece of wood placed between two chairs; I also used old bicycle tire tubes as exercise bands.

Despite our limited knowledge of proper exercise techniques, Bob and I agreed to follow the routines three times a week. I soon realized the power of having a workout buddy. Whenever I felt lazy, Bob would motivate me, and vice versa. We provided each other with encouragement and accountability. While we never graced the pages of *Muscle and Fitness Magazine*, we had a fantastic time, gained valuable exercise experience, and learned about bodybuilding. Additionally, I discovered the importance of positive support, reinforcement, encouragement, and, when necessary, the occasional nagging or kick in the butt. Both of us still lift weights.

Margo Chevers

I can guarantee that I would not have finished my first book in 2007 without my monthly meetings with Margo Chevers, my goal buddy from 2006 to 2013. Margo was a professional speaker, trainer, author, and consultant. Every month, we met for one and a half hours to review our accomplishments, set new goals, discuss and share ideas, and serve as cheerleaders for each other.

As part of our monthly process, we would discuss each other's goals, write our individual goals for the month, and keep a copy of each other's goal lists. This way, we both knew what the other was expected to do. The goal list forced us to think about what we would do over the next month and to set our priorities. It kept us committed.

Sometimes, we knew we could accomplish more than what was on our list, and other times, when things like vacations and workshops meant we might accomplish a little less, the key was to learn to stretch without becoming overwhelmed. Most of all, it kept us moving forward.

Another critical aspect of our arrangement was that we never missed a monthly meeting. Getting off track is too easy. We initially had several people who wanted to be part of our group; we intended to have four or five members, but several people who said they wanted to join kept pushing us off. So, we decided we were better off moving forward with just the two of us rather than having people who were not committed.

A key to having a goal buddy or mastermind group is a commitment to yourself and your partners. Sometimes, I would complete my goals fifteen minutes before we met, yet I always finished. I also know what goals to set and how much I can do. I understand that if I overcommit, I will be in trouble, and if I undercommit, what's the point? At the end of each meeting, we would exchange $500 checks, each made payable to the other and post-dated until the next meeting. If we did not complete our goals, the other could cash the check and spend the $500! (No checks needed to be cashed in those seven years!)

The saying "You can't see the forest for the trees" is a time-honored adage rich with insight. Often, when we encounter challenges, we struggle to step back and grasp the overall situation. In navigating life's complexities, we often find ourselves entrenched among numerous distractions, unable to perceive anything beyond the immediate hurdles in our path.

Having mentors, coaches, goal buddies, or a mastermind group offers you a different perspective. These individuals are not involved and have no personal interests at stake. They are not emotionally involved, so they don't have the same attachments.

They can see things you cannot or are unwilling to see. By offering a different, more neutral perspective, they often help us make better decisions. Over time, your mastermind group will come to know you—The Good, the Bad, and the Ugly.

They will know when you are procrastinating, succeeding, or struggling. They will help you stay on track and motivated.

Top Guns

There are different types of Mastermind groups, and one that I was part of for ten years was called "Top Guns." This monthly sales group was based on the Sandler Sales System and comprised only individuals who had undergone the System's training and supported its concepts.

Each month, group members shared their sales strategies, successes, and struggles, and they received feedback from the group. This group taught me the power of negative consequences, which Margo and I applied. Many managers, including myself, dislike giving reviews. This may be due to an old saying we've heard from our parents: "If you can't say anything nice, don't say anything at all." However, that approach is counterproductive and may hurt more people than it helps. So, here's what I did: I promised the group that if I did not complete my employee reviews by the next meeting, which was 30 days away, I would give the group $250 to do as they wished. In those days, $250 was equivalent to about $750 today. Guess what? I completed the reviews within a week, demonstrating the power of being in a group and the potential negative consequences.

Frankie D.

Frankie D—a friend of mine, as well as a professional speaker, trainer, and magician—decided it was time to lose weight and get in shape. Instead of going it alone, he teamed up with a friend who shared the same goal. Together, they made a pact to stay committed, holding each other accountable with daily check-ins via phone or email. Did it work? Absolutely. To the best of my knowledge, both of them are still in great shape years later.

This simple story proves just how powerful accountability can be. It doesn't require anything fancy—just someone to show up for and report to. Accountability is one of the most effective and accessible tools we have for achieving and maintaining lasting change. Why go it alone when progress is easier—and a lot more fun—when shared?

Find A Way Mastermind

For over a decade, I facilitated a monthly Mastermind group composed of diverse individuals—executives, small business owners, and administrators—all of whom had completed my six-week *Find-A-Way* workshop. That was their ticket into the group. At any given time, we had between five and eight active members, and together, we accomplished some incredible things: launching businesses, earning advanced degrees and certifications, paying off significant debt, and completing major life and career projects.

Here's what's interesting: over 100 people took the workshop, but only a small percentage joined the Mastermind group afterward. Why? Because most people quit too soon. They attend a workshop, feel inspired, and maybe even take the first step—but when the excitement fades, so does the effort.

One of my favorite quotes has sat on my desk for over 30 years.

> *"Success seems to be largely a matter of hanging on after others have let go."*
>
> — William Feather, 20th century industrialist

It's true. The ones who stuck with the group made real progress—not because they were smarter or more talented, but because they kept showing up and stayed accountable.

Through this group, I saw the power of accountability in action. Some of the philosophies in this book—like the *Annual Letter to Self* or having a partner sign off on your goals (or pay up if you don't follow through)—were born in that Mastermind room. We had to get creative. Even committed members could become complacent, so we built in new strategies to keep the momentum alive.

Never underestimate what a small group of focused people can do. Most of us already know what we need to do; we just don't *do it*. I once told the group, "If I don't finish my employee reviews before next month's meeting, I won't do them at all." That's accountability with teeth.

Finally, one of my biggest oversights was forgetting to include a favorite quote by Charles "Tremendous" Jones in an early draft of this book. Don't make the same mistake I did—memorize it, live it:

"You are the same today as you'll be in five years, except for two things: the people you meet and the books you read."

Read that again. And again. Because it's simple—and it's everything.

> *"You will be the same person in five years as you are today except for the people you meet and the books you read."*
>
> — Charlie "Tremendous" Jones

I would add, "the people with whom you associate, and **the actions you take**."

2

Who Am I Really? A Hilarious Journey to Self-Discovery

An often-overlooked essential lesson is the power of one's belief system. One's beliefs about life, money, and the world shape one's self-understanding.

You may have even said this yourself or heard others say, "Oh, that's just the way I am." No, it is the way you choose to be, and much of that occurs on an unconscious level. This is why paying attention to and knowing yourself, your beliefs, and how you operate is important. Your beliefs govern your successes and failures, where you live, whom you marry, what you think about the world, and whether you believe you can or cannot do certain things.

Understanding what you believe is essential, especially when working toward success. Your beliefs will either move you forward or hold you back. This is why being in a group can be a great experience. You can hear and see the results of others' beliefs, which may prompt you to question your own beliefs and actions, leading to changes. Remember: isolation is the enemy of success, and receiving good feedback is essential.

Know who you are and know what you want

"Knowing yourself is the beginning of all wisdom."

— Aristotle

Jack Canfield once said, "We are afraid to want what we want." Consider this statement and reflect on what you allow yourself to want or not want, as well as what you truly desire. Ask yourself, "If that is what I want, what is stopping me?" Could it be old messages I'm carrying around, such as "What Other People Think" or "I can't do that"?

Many times, when we think or say, "I want to _____," our minds bombard us with chatter, bringing up fears and doubts. It's crucial to have self-awareness and clarity about what you want, as well as to be aware of the chatter. Decision-making can be complex when considering what you truly want. People often avoid it because they fear not liking what they have committed to. However, it's essential to remember that it's perfectly fine to change your mind, adjust, or go in a different direction if something doesn't work out. The key is to get out of your own way and start trying.

What stops you from doing what you like and want?

Achieving self-knowledge requires personal responsibility and attention, not only to who you are now but also to who you were in the past, who you aspire to be, and your tendencies, even as a child, a teenager, and a young adult.

1. What did you like?
2. What interested you?
3. What seemed easier and came naturally?
4. What is easy for you to do or understand?

Sometimes, others see us better. Here's a personal example. Every year, during my annual goal-setting ritual, I ask one of my mentors, Dave Rothfeld, "Dave, what should I do to improve my business?"

And every year, without missing a beat, Dave replies, "Dennis, hire a manager — and you go sell."

The following year, the same question yields the same answer: "Dennis, hire a manager — and you sell."

It took me a long time to understand what he was really saying. I call that self-defeating behavior — or maybe just being chicken. Was it fear that held me back? Probably. The fear of losing control, even though managing wasn't exactly my strength. The fear of "What if it doesn't work?"

The truth is, we all have to examine what holds us back. Often, it's not circumstances— it's the unspoken, unexamined beliefs that stir up fear and doubt. Pay close attention to your "what-ifs." They're like signposts, pointing directly to the stories we tell ourselves — stories that quietly limit our potential.

The sooner we confront those beliefs, the sooner we can move forward.

Here is food for thought: How often have you held yourself back for fear of judgment or being perceived as arrogant? Always remember, it's your life, goals, and dreams. This is another reason to be conscious and deliberate about who is in your group, personal club, and environment.

To achieve our full potential and identify areas that need focus, it is essential to reflect on our beliefs and acknowledge our doubts and fears. Furthermore, there may be aspects of ourselves that we are unable or unwilling to see, but that others may see. In such situations, seeking advice from trusted individuals can be beneficial, and this is where the group becomes valuable.

Pay attention to patterns that move you forward or hold you back; these are the areas to capitalize on, fix, improve, or avoid. Ask yourself the following questions:

1. Why do I react this way?
2. Why do I think this way?
3. Is this an unwanted belief that someone has instilled in me?
4. Do I understand that obstacles always accompany the path to success?
5. How or when did I become this way, or when did I start thinking this way?
6. What mistakes or self-defeating behaviors do I keep repeating?

Both individuals and group members need to understand their strengths and weaknesses.

Embracing Weaknesses: The First Step to Real Growth

Acknowledging your weaknesses isn't a sign of failure; it's a bold act of self-awareness and the first step toward real, lasting growth. While it can be uncomfortable to confront where we fall short, doing so opens the door to learning, progress, and meaningful change.

It takes humility and courage to admit limitations, but honesty allows you to set more realistic goals, make better decisions, and approach challenges with confidence. When you accept your vulnerabilities, you also empower yourself to seek support, ask better questions, collaborate more effectively, and take smarter actions.

Recognizing your shortcomings doesn't make you less capable; it makes you more resilient. It shows you're willing to grow, adapt, and improve. And that's where transformation begins.

Remember: nobody gets stronger by pretending they have no weaknesses. Growth starts with the truth—and the truth is that owning your flaws is one of the most powerful things you can do.

Tools

You can take personality profiles, such as the Myers-Briggs Personality Profile or the Gallup StrengthsFinder, as examples that provide insight into your style and offer valuable clues. While these profiles may not have all the answers, they serve as a strong starting point. We often neglect to pay attention to ourselves, think deeply, or dismiss our weaknesses and strengths.

Particularly regarding strengths, we frequently take them for granted and either fail to acknowledge or minimize them. Both individuals and groups need to understand their strengths and weaknesses to unlock their full potential.

What Color is Your Parachute?

The *What Color Is Your Parachute?* workbook is based on the original book of the same name, first published in 1972 by Richard Bolles. This popular book has sold over 10 million copies worldwide. Bolles's extensive workbook will help you discover more about yourself, including your skills, potential, and value. The workbook contains numerous exercises designed to encourage you to think critically and gain a deeper understanding of yourself.

The Golden Triangle

The Golden Triangle serves as a valuable framework for gaining a deeper understanding of oneself. It encompasses an examination of your interests and passions, your unique talents and skills, and your inherent abilities. Furthermore, it is crucial to evaluate the financial feasibility and potential income streams associated with your selected path. This process demands deliberate effort and thoughtful decision-making to refine your choices and hone in on what genuinely resonates with you. Below is a visual depiction of this triangle.

GOLDEN TRIANGLE

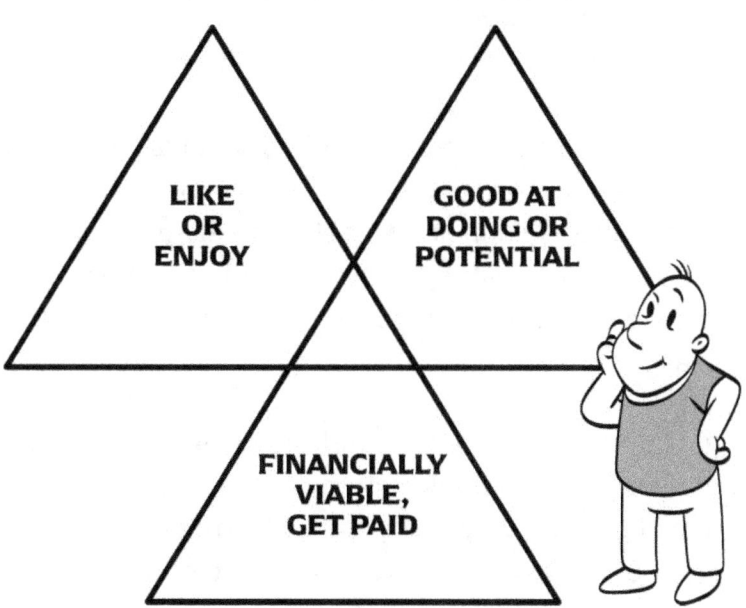

Here is an example of how you can use the Golden Triangle to help you know yourself better:

1. **Identify your interests or passions**: Consider what truly brings you joy and fulfillment. These can be hobbies, activities, aspects of work, or subjects you enjoy exploring.
2. **Assess your talents and skills**: Reflect on what you are naturally good at and what you can further develop. These may include technical skills, creative abilities, or practical talents. Don't underestimate your capabilities and potential.

3. **Reflect on your unique qualities or strengths** to determine your innate abilities. These can be personal traits, intellectual capabilities, or intuitive gifts.
4. **Evaluate financial viability**: Analyze how your interests, talents, and potential abilities can translate into a financially viable career, business, or source of income. Research market demand and possible opportunities that align with your skills and interests.

By exploring these facets and identifying the overlap between your interests, strengths, potential, and financial prospects, you can gain a deeper understanding of yourself and make well-informed choices about your future.

Consider the case of an individual who prefers interpersonal interactions, enjoys variety, and thrives on movement throughout their day. In this scenario, careers such as computer programming or accounting would not be suitable. Instead, roles like outside sales, bartending, law enforcement, entrepreneurship, emergency medical technician, or stand-up comedy might align more closely with their preferences and lifestyle.

DENNIS A. McCURDY

Abraham Maslow, the American psychologist, offers these insights.

True change begins when we courageously face the extraordinary potential that lies within. W*hat a person can be, they must be*— this is the essence of self-actualization. A musician must create music, an artist must paint, and a poet must write to find true inner peace. Yet too often, people sell themselves short, settling for less than their full capacity. When we cling to one narrow way of seeing the world — like the man or woman who only has a hammer — we limit our growth. Lasting happiness demands that we embrace both our flaws and our god-like possibilities.

> *"There are three things that are extremely hard: steel, a diamond, and to know oneself."*
>
> — Benjamin Franklin

3

Mission Impossible? Setting Goals I Might Actually Reach

I'm wealthy beyond my wildest dreams! Unfortunately, my dreams were never very wild.

Goals are like GPS for your life—without them, you're just driving in circles, hoping to land somewhere good.

> *"The greatest danger for most of us is not that our aim is too high and we miss it, but that it is too low, and we reach it."*
>
> — Michelangelo

Goals are a path to follow to a destination, a guide for activity.

They give your actions direction, help you focus, and keep you from getting lost in distractions (or Netflix marathons). But here's the tricky part: getting clear on what you want isn't always easy. That's why vague goals like "get in shape" or "make more money" don't cut it.

You've got to be specific. Why? Because specific goals make it easier to create a plan, track your wins, and celebrate your progress instead of wondering, *"Am I even getting anywhere?"*

Set clear goals. Make a plan. Take action. Then high-five yourself for being a goal-crushing rockstar.

Once you have identified your goals, the next step is to break them down into smaller, manageable steps called Micro Goals (Steps). Prioritize these steps and be clear about what needs to be done to accomplish them. Clarity is crucial because it helps you understand your priorities. By reflecting on what you have done or have been doing, you can see what matters most to you. Therefore, it is essential to set clear goals and steps to ensure that you are making progress toward achieving what truly matters to you. When we don't have clear goals and a plan, we aren't really planning.

Accountability is also key to this process; having a supportive Mastermind Group can provide the necessary guidance and encouragement to keep you on track. They will help you stay focused and motivated and provide the support you need to achieve your goals. It is important to note that you don't necessarily have to complete your goals or planning if your objective is to create them while working in your Mastermind Group as part of your process.

Clarity is essential because it provides you with the steps in your process. The best approach is to have a detailed plan of action and a strategy that includes possible obstacles and **STEPs** (**S**pecific **T**argeted **E**ffort **P**lan). This should serve as your action plan as much as possible. By "detailed," I mean enough information to ensure certainty about what, when, where, with whom, the steps involved, and how long it will take to accomplish your goal.

This will be important as you will have Mastermind group check-ins and checkpoints. In other words, if you declare it, you must do it.

The statement "I want to improve my health" is not a specific enough goal to be effective. Here is an example of a concrete, tangible goal.

Here's an example of a clear and concrete goal:

I will walk three miles and lift weights for 30 minutes at 7:30 AM on Monday, Wednesday, Friday, and Saturday.

The goal is to improve my health. Expanded version:

- I will lose 20 pounds by September 1st, 20xx. (This is not a good plan if you set this goal in August.)
- By next Tuesday (date) of next week, I will join the local gym (name).
- I will meet with a trainer and receive coaching within seven days of joining.

- I will find a workout buddy within two weeks of joining the gym.
- I will go to the gym at 7:30 AM on Mondays, Wednesdays, Fridays, and Saturdays.
- I will use the sauna at least twice weekly after my workout.
- I will listen to YouTube videos or attend a class on healthy eating within ten days of starting my program, and I will continue to listen and learn for the rest of my life.
- I will count and track calories each day.
- I will weigh in every Friday.

KISSES is a Concept/Tool that Can Help with Any Goal

KISSES is one of the powerful concepts I wrote about in my book *Suck It Up, Cupcake, Stop Screwing Yourself, and Get the Life You Want*. KISSES stands for:

- **K**eep (Promise-Vow)
- **I**t (The goal or objective)
- **S**mall (small enough so it's hard to find excuses not to do something)
- **S**ustainable (never underestimate the power and importance of sustainability)
- **E**asy (the easier it is to do and repeat, the better)

- **S**upported (Mastermind Group, coach, accountability partner—important)

The concept of KISSES is to keep your goals small and sustainable. This means making them easy (achievable) and supported. If your goals are too large or set for too short a time frame, you may fall into the all-or-nothing trap. This is a typical self-defeating behavior where you set huge goals and end up doing or achieving nothing because the steps toward your goal are unsustainable, leaving you overwhelmed. It's essential to develop the habit of setting small and achievable goals. Remember, little hinges swing big doors.

Making it easy means making it convenient, including the time of day, location, and anything you can do to ensure you follow through. Being supported is also crucial.

Having a workout buddy or accountability partner can make a significant difference. People with a workout partner and support tend to stick to their programs longer and work harder. Remember, we tend to perform better when someone is watching us.

> *"For every level, there is another devil."*
>
> — Tyrese Gibson

UNLEASH THE POWER OF CONNECTION

What does *"for every level, there is another devil"* mean? It means that every time you try to grow, change, or do something new, you will face obstacles, challenges, uncertainty, doubt, and fear. Whenever we grow, there is another devil. We must move past our comfort zone, being aware and remembering what Mark Twain said: "Comfort makes cowards of us all." Once we reach a certain point, we may need to step out of our comfort zone to move forward. If we're not moving forward, we're neutral; truthfully, we're usually moving backward.

When it comes to comfort, habits, and goals, this is what Michelangelo said: *"The greatest danger for most of us is not that our aim is too high and we miss it, but that it is too low and we reach it."*

Whew—that hits a nerve. It might sound a little intimidating, but here's the good news: it's not as scary as it seems. Reaching big goals doesn't mean doing big things all at once. It's about breaking them down into bite-sized steps—**tiny** actions you can take every day.

Think of it this way: Success isn't a giant leap; it's a series of small steps.

"If you go to work on your goals, your goals will go to work on you."

— Jim Rohn

Conflicting Goals

People often worry about money, security, or health, yet their actions directly oppose achieving those goals. Examples:

Health: skimping on food quality, eating fast food, overeating, not counting calories, not exercising, drinking excessively, and partying too much.

Money and security: wasting money on things they don't need, buying something more expensive than necessary, and not saving or investing for their future. These are just a few of the many types of conflicting goals, also known as *self-sabotage*.

"One of the main reasons many people struggle with goals is there is no feedback loop. Feedback is the nuts and bolts of your goals."

— Dennis A. McCurdy

Many individuals express a desire to become more organized, yet they frequently misplace their keys, important documents, and tools. This often occurs because they lack designated spaces for these items or fail to consistently return them to their proper locations. It's an all-too-common issue.

According to *Lost and Found Statistics*, the average American spends 2.5 days (60 hours) per year looking for their belongings. Remember, that is only an *average*. The result is a daily, never-ending scavenger hunt. This is a classic example of self-defeating behavior. More importantly, they lose time—something they can never get back. Time! If you live 60 years in adulthood, that amounts to 3,600 hours, which is about half a year. The more time you spend looking for things, the less you have to accomplish important tasks. Some people mistakenly believe that time spent organizing is a waste. In reality, disorganization often leads to lost time, frustration, and added stress for themselves and those around them. In a sense, this mindset can also be seen as a subtle form of procrastination.

Other time-wasters include excessive TV watching, computer scrolling, and engaging in activities that do not contribute to accomplishing goals. What is considered excessive? If the important tasks that move you forward aren't getting done, that's excessive. Start by gradually reducing distractions or self-defeating behaviors, and don't go cold turkey; that rarely works.

> *"You Can Have Almost Everything You Want, Though Not Usually Simultaneously."*

We often engage in self-sabotage through conflicting goals, trying to accomplish or acquire too much at once. This approach rarely works unless you have someone to delegate tasks to. Having too many goals can lead to bottlenecks, frustration, anxiety, and, ultimately, failure. A Mastermind Group, goal buddy, or accountability partner can be invaluable in helping you narrow your focus. They can provide an outside perspective, hold you accountable, and prevent you from overloading yourself, which helps avoid the pitfalls of failure.

Beware of conflicting or excessive goals as a form of self-sabotaging behavior!

Additionally, be aware that some people overload themselves so that if they fail, they have an excuse. Many individuals fear failure, while others fear success. Focusing on one or two significant goals can be challenging. There's an old saying: "A hunter who chases two rabbits catches none." I am not a big fan of this saying; in fact, I dislike it because I prefer to chase many rabbits, even though it rarely works.

UNLEASH THE POWER OF CONNECTION

Focus can be difficult for some people, and I know I am one of them. This is where your support team comes into play. You can count on them to call you out and help you rein yourself in when you are out of control, and even better, *before* you get out of control.

Pay attention and learn to recognize when you are beginning to engage in self-defeating behavior patterns, such as overloading yourself. It is also common for people to fall prey to these: FOMO, or Fear of Missing Out, and SOS, or Shiny Object Syndrome. As I mentioned earlier, you can do almost anything, just not simultaneously.

When we notice these behaviors, it is a sign that it is time to prioritize. Push less important goals down the road for later.

This way, you're not giving them up; you are simply postponing them. At some point, you may need to weed through your garden of goals and eliminate some of them because they will not serve you in the long run.

> *"First, say to yourself what you would be, and then do what you must do."*
>
> — Epictetus

4

The Valley of Dead Dreams: When Goals Get Tangled in Reality

> *"Many of us are haunted by the ghost of things left undone—goals unfulfilled, and potential never realized."*
>
> — Dennis A. McCurdy

The *Valley of Dead Dreams* is where ambitions go to die. It's the danger zone between inspiration, execution, and completion. It's where dreams stall, and where we need the most support, accountability, and, let's be honest—a good kick in the ass.

It's easy to get stuck in the valley. The initial excitement fades, the dopamine from your shiny new goal disappears, and it's just you and the work. The grind. No more rush—just resistance. But that's also when the real magic *can* happen if you don't quit.

Let's face it: no one is always on their game or motivated. We all have times when we are tired, discouraged, lazy, stay up too late, attend way too many parties, and want to quit. It happens to all of us. I'm also saying that sometimes you must take time off to regroup and rejuvenate. That's a given. At times, we need to suck it up and push through. Who's there to help? Your Mastermind Group, accountability partner, coach, or mentor. They will ensure that you don't stay down too long.

UNLEASH THE POWER OF CONNECTION

Recently, I was helping a friend who is a psychologist. He's intelligent and has created many good writings, but that's where it always ends. He gets caught in the Valley of Dead Dreams. What do I mean?

He does the work, sets it aside, works on another project, and sets that aside, but he never follows through with moving his efforts forward. We recently discussed a piece he wrote around ten years ago, which sold a thousand copies but then fell off.

When he pulled out the original, he realized it was thirty years old. He could have done much with that work and helped many people, but he got caught in the *Valley of Dead Dreams*. This is also when we must learn to delegate to find someone to move our project forward. This goes back to knowing who you are, your strengths and weaknesses, and overcoming your weaknesses.

You *Valley of Dead Dreams* all have a classic car that has been sitting there for ten years, waiting to be started: the partially finished addition, the half-painted house, or the half-completed garden.

Someday!

> *"There are seven days in a week, and "someday" is not one of them."*
>
> — Benny Lewis

It's essential to recognize that the most challenging part of any journey is often the middle, which can be a lengthy and arduous stretch. The beginning and end are usually shorter than the time and effort required to achieve your goal or implement your idea. You should anticipate facing obstacles and setbacks during this phase, which I call the "Valley of Dead Dreams." Planning for this part of the journey is crucial because it is an inevitable aspect of any project. The length and depth of this valley can vary depending on the size and originality of the project, and it could last for months, years, or even decades. We often start working on a project with enthusiasm and energy, but then we encounter challenges such as boredom, tedious work, setbacks, and long hours with little progress. This is when we need support and motivation the most. Having a Mastermind Group, a goal buddy, and an accountability partner or coach is important to help us push through this challenging phase.

UNLEASH THE POWER OF CONNECTION

If you're like most people, you need a lot of support in the valley. Did I say a lot? I mean a ton. Make it part of your plan to build your TEAM, aka GANG, and get things done.

> *"If you really want to do something, you'll find a way. If you don't; you'll find an excuse."*
>
> — Jim Rohn

5

From Idea to Action: How Mastermind Groups Dive Results

> *"We will disappoint ourselves before we disappoint another. This is human nature."*
>
> — Simon Sinek

Most of us know what to do; we just don't do it.

Why do mastermind groups work? Well, that is, as the old game show host used to say, "The $64,000 Question" (which is also the show's name). Humans are tribal, and our need for social connection is ingrained and powerful. Our ancestors needed to be part of a tribe or group to survive. Long ago, most tribes were small; research indicates an average community size of 5 to 80 people, later expanding to as many as 150. The communities were tight-knit, and everyone depended on each other to pull their weight and uphold their tribe's values and codes. Being ostracized from the tribe was not just a punishment; it was a matter of life or death. Even in more modern times, one of the worst punishments is banishment—exile from your group or peers, excommunication, being canceled, or solitary confinement. You could say that being part of a tribe or group is in our DNA and is essential to our survival, both physically and emotionally. Today, it isn't the danger of physical harm but rather emotional harm that we face. This is where the power of a Mastermind Group comes in. It's a tribe, a community, that provides accountability and, to a certain degree, safety.

Interestingly, the people we associate with can rewire our brains. Individuals will completely change their behavior in a group setting. Consider cults, where people engage in insane and irrational actions to belong. Mastermind Groups harness that propensity to create positive change.

Joining a Mastermind Group can be intimidating. New challenges naturally bring some doubt and fear—the fear of not being accepted, of failing, of looking bad, and of not living up to the group's expectations.

Those who move past these fears tend to do better and succeed. In the long run, the group will help you overcome fear, doubt, and self-defeating behaviors, and it can also instill a dose of courage.

You must be careful about whom you follow and who influences you. Never underestimate the power of a group. People will betray their values or sabotage themselves to gain acceptance and a sense of belonging. You see this in street gangs, where, for little or nothing, young men often put their lives in danger solely for the privilege of being part of a gang.

UNLEASH THE POWER OF CONNECTION

Once someone is in a group, most people will work hard to remain in that group. Being part of an empowering group, such as a Mastermind Group, and harnessing the power of the need to belong is highly beneficial for anyone willing to open themselves up to growth. You may have heard this sage advice: "Show me your friends, and I will show you your future."

> *"The fault, dear Brutus, is not in our stars but in ourselves that we are underlings."*
>
> — William Shakespeare Julius Caesar; Act 1 Cassius to Brutus

This is a critical learning mechanism that begins in childhood but extends beyond it. Mirror neurons prompt us to observe and replicate the actions and emotions of others. For instance, when we see someone smiling, we are inclined to smile as well. These mirror neurons are activated not only when we experience emotions ourselves but also when we observe others experiencing feelings such as happiness, fear, anger, sadness, or courage.

What is Cassius saying? He is telling Brutus that it is within us, not fate, the stars, or luck, and that it is up to us to take charge of our lives and find our own way.

Mirror Neurons

We have neurons in our brains called mirror neurons. Mirror neurons are responsible for triggering the imitation or emulation of other people's behaviors. They are a powerful learning tool—not just in childhood, but throughout life. They help us mimic the actions and emotions of others. That's why, when someone smiles at us, we often smile back without even thinking. These neurons fire both when we feel an emotion and when we see someone else feeling it—whether it's joy, fear, anger, sadness, or even courage. It's our brain's way of saying, "I feel you."

As we mature and become more independent, we must be mindful of the individuals we choose to emulate. When we reflect on our lives, we can consider the impact that the people in our social circles have had on us. For instance, did you exercise more when you spent time with physically active individuals?

We automatically mirror the behaviors of those around us, and they do the same.

Paying attention is essential; that is, being clear about what you want. Being clear about your desires serves as a guide to the people with whom you should associate and whom you want to emulate.

The Propinquity Effect: Why Closeness Creates Influence

"Propinquity" might sound like a term you'd find in a dusty psychology textbook, but it's a game-changer once you understand it. At its core, it simply means *nearness*—physical, emotional, or psychological closeness. Whether in person or online, the more likely we are to build connections, develop trust, and even *start thinking and behaving like those around us*.

We don't decide to conform—it just happens, quietly and powerfully.

This is known as the **Propinquity Effect**, and it operates mostly beneath the surface of our awareness. We unconsciously start to mirror the norms, habits, and goals of the people we see most often. It's not about weakness—it's human nature. Evolution has wired us to follow the group because, for most of history, survival depended on it.

That's why your environment—where you live, work, and socialize—matters more than you think. The group you're surrounded by will shape your thinking. It will pull you toward its center of gravity. That can be a blessing or a trap, depending on whom you allow into your orbit.

So here's the takeaway: be intentional about whom and what you keep close. Proximity isn't just a matter of geography; it's about influence. Whether you're chasing big goals or trying to change old habits, the people and places you allow into your daily life can either fuel your momentum or quietly stall your progress.

Choose consciously, because whether you realize it or not, the group rules..

Things Change as We Grow

Life is a continual process. Life changes, and goals change. Sometimes, we need to find different associations, but this doesn't mean we must abandon or discard our old relationships. However, we may need to reevaluate or limit some relationships. We must be judicious about how much time we spend and with whom we spend it. There are people with whom I will occasionally have a beer, and that's it. If you associate with people who don't align with your goals, they will draw you into their goals, and it's even worse if they don't have any goals.

Here is some sage wisdom: "You can't soar with the eagles if you hang out with turkeys." I don't know who said this first, so let's attribute it to Anonymous, a great Stoic philosopher.

UNLEASH THE POWER OF CONNECTION

It is a matter of paying attention and understanding that not everyone has goals or the drive to succeed. Many people are content where they are. Alan Laiken, the author of *How to Get Control of Your Time and Your Life,* reminds us to "Be selfish with your time and kind to people." In other words, protect your most valuable resource: time. But don't be a jerk.

You can see why understanding mirror neurons and how your brain works is essential to the Mastermind concept: we see and do likewise. These concepts help when we feel stuck, distracted, or lazy. So, take heed. Few people possess incredible discipline and willpower. We need someone in our corner to nudge and push us.

Personally, I hate to be pushed, yet I appreciate the results. Right now, I am struggling with the 400-word writing goal I have set for myself each day. The index card with the tick marks is staring at me. I can picture Clint Eastwood in the 1983 movie *Sudden Impact,* with that index card saying, "Go ahead, make my day," which translates to "0" for the day—no results, a failure—rather than a slash for completed.

Recently, I met with a young writer who is struggling. I am helping him get out of his own way, push past excuses, and write. I encouraged him to pick a tiny writing target that he could accomplish daily, no matter what, reminding him that "a little every day goes a long way." Until now, his daily writing goal had been too big, and guess what?

Nothing happened. Nothing got written.

When we think the goal is too big, we self-sabotage and may say, "Oh, what's the use?" All too often, when we think all or nothing, we get nothing!

There are many books on thinking big to win. You know the saying, "Go big or go home." Yet most people never reach their goals. Why? Because they think too big and then panic, feel overwhelmed, self-sabotage, or make excuses. Rather than having a tiny, attainable micro goal and succeeding, they create huge plans and do nothing. It becomes, "I don't have time for all that right now." What about doing 10 minutes now? Your Mastermind Group will help you set achievable goals and overcome inertia. The key is that the goals must be sustainable and attainable. In the case of my young writer mentee, he is keeping the goal small and within reach, knowing the potential obstacles and developing a plan to get past them. There will be fewer obstacles and excuses if the goal is small enough.

Teamwork

To demonstrate the power of teams and groups, in 2005, my son Adam was a member of the rowing team at the Rochester Institute of Technology. When a friend asked him why he got up at 4:15 in the morning to be in a boat by 5:30 AM in the cold, he wrote the following in his email's away message. I titled it "WHY."

> "Why? Because every morning, I wake up with the knowledge that it is one day closer to the moment when I will sit in a boat poised at three-quarters slide; in front of and behind me there will be others who have worked just as hard as I have, who have been waiting just as long for this moment. Across the water, there will be another; he too will have forsaken his name for a number, and he too will be sitting ready at three-quarters slide. I do it because I know at that moment that I need to be better than him; I know that eight other people depend on me to be better than him, and I will not be the person to let them down."
>
> — Adam D. McCurdy

The power of commitment to others lies in the way it transforms personal motivation into collective responsibility.

Adam's message perfectly captures this. He didn't wake up at 4:15 AM in the freezing cold just for himself; he did it because others were counting on him. His individual effort wasn't isolated; it was woven into the fabric of a team, and the success of the whole depended on the strength and dedication of each part.

Here's why commitment to others is so powerful:

- **It raises your standards.** You'll work harder for your team than you might for yourself. When you know others rely on you, "good enough" isn't good enough.
- **It builds resilience.** Cold mornings, fatigue, and doubt become easier to push through when you're doing it for something bigger than yourself.
- **It creates accountability.** You don't want to be the weak link. That sense of duty drives you to show up, even when it's hard.
- **It deepens purpose.** The goal becomes more meaningful when it's shared. You're no longer chasing a personal win; you're part of a shared pursuit, a bond.

Adam's "WHY" reminds us that true strength doesn't just come from within; it comes from the bond we share with others and the promise we make not to let them down. That's the heartbeat of teamwork.

UNLEASH THE POWER OF CONNECTION

That's the power of commitment.

6

Mastermind: The Secret Sauce for Success

"People need help and support toward every goal."

— Lewis Mehl-Madrona, MD, author of Coyote Healing

My original title for this book was "The Magic of Mastermind" because adopting the philosophies and processes outlined in this book will feel like magic. A good mastermind group, goal buddy, accountability partner, mentor, or coach is magical if we open ourselves to the process. Embracing this process can be frightening or exhilarating, but you'll be eternally grateful.

We must understand that our brains prioritize energy conservation and safety. Whether we achieve great success or pursue our aspirations holds no significance for our minds. This evolutionary development occurred between 35,000 and 100,000 years ago, with the singular aim of ensuring our survival. Despite viewing ourselves as advanced and intellectual beings, our brains have not kept pace with this evolution. However, we can harness our innate tribal instincts and the power of collaboration to move forward effectively.

I've learned the hard way that not everyone who agrees with you is doing you a favor.

UNLEASH THE POWER OF CONNECTION

Early on, I used to take people at their word—if they said an idea was great, I believed it. If they said, "Keep going, you're doing fine," I assumed I was on track. But over time, I realized something important: many people aren't trying to mislead you—they're just trying to be kind. They soften the truth because they don't want to hurt your feelings. The problem is that sugarcoating reality doesn't change reality. I've wasted time, lost money, and added too much stress to my life by trusting feedback that prioritized being nice over being real.

That's why today, I value a support system built on genuine encouragement, true integrity, and loyalty that doesn't flinch when the truth needs to be told. Honest feedback might sting, but it can save you years.

Mastermind groups are effective. Even skeptics soon realize the positive and powerful impact that the group can have on their lives, businesses, and careers. Here are additional gaps and struggles that your mastermind group will help you address:

- Avoid denial.
- Set better goals, be clear, and cut through excuses.
- Be accountable.
- Stop procrastinating.

- Find support when you need it.
- Be encouraged, and you will encourage others.
- Find more courage.
- Move faster.
- Think bigger.
- Gain confidence.
- Increase creativity.
- Discover new options.
- Make better decisions.
- Avoid making mistakes or make fewer of them.
- View things from a different perspective.
- Gain the combined experience of all the people in the group and their individual experiences.
- Find satisfaction in helping group members.
- Learn by listening to the challenges, struggles, and solutions of others.
- Recognize yourself in the mistakes, fears, and misgivings of others.
- Understand your strengths and weaknesses.

A Mastermind Group will work for you if you put in the effort. Remember the Beatles' song, "I get by with a little help from my friends."

"We will always be smarter than me."

— Dennis A. McCurdy

7

The Case for Collaboration: Why Mastermind Groups Matter

The Eaglets

"Come to the edge," he said. "We can't, we're afraid!" they responded.

"Come to the edge," he said.

"We can't, we will fall!" they responded.

"Come to the edge," he said.

And so they came. And he pushed them.

And they flew."

— Guillaume Apollinaire

The Mastermind Group

What is a Mastermind Group? A Mastermind Group is a collection of individuals with a common goal and a desire to succeed, improve their lives, businesses, or careers, and grow personally. Individuals can form Mastermind Groups from the same company, among entrepreneurs, within the same industry, or with anyone seeking personal improvement. While direct competitors can participate, it may be best to avoid doing so.

Does it cost to join a Mastermind Group? It may, but usually not if you start one or join a small group. If there is a cost, consider it an investment rather than an expense. Why is it an investment? Any positive changes you make are a worthwhile investment in yourself, and they will compound; they are yours forever.

Who Has Had a Mastermind Group?

The concept of Mastermind Groups has existed for a long time. Few people succeed in a vacuum; most successful individuals have some form of a Mastermind Group. Here are just a few examples:

- Corporate boards of directors
- The President's Cabinet
- Psychologist peer review groups
- Financial advisors' study groups You may have heard the story of

Mastermind Groups in Napoleon Hill's 1937 book *Think and Grow Rich*. The Mastermind Groups he referred to were known as "The Master Mind Alliances." Sometime in the 1920s, Andrew Carnegie and five others formed an alliance called the Big 6, and they were not the only ones or the first. Benjamin Franklin gathered the same friends every Friday night to discuss morals, politics, and philosophy. The group was named the Junto Club, also known as the Leather Apron Club, and it ran for 38 years. The group eventually became the American Philosophical Society.

The four vagabonds—Henry Ford, Thomas Edison, Harvey Firestone, and naturalist John Burroughs—set out to improve the American road travel experience and safety. The group continued for ten years.

Dorothy Parker was a member of the Algonquin Round Table, a group of writers, poets, and critics, from 1919 to 1929.

In recent years, comedians Adam Sandler, Kevin James, David Spade, and Chris Rock have worked together in comedy. The possibilities are endless. All these individuals in the group shared their insights and helped each other grow and develop.

People may have multiple Mastermind Groups, some for business, hobbies, or personal development, depending on their individual needs. The point is to share, learn, and develop from each other's experiences. The key here is to use your imagination.

You can have a group for almost anything you want to do or improve. There are various levels of groups, ranging from beginners to advanced. It is all about being open to exploring and developing yourself and the other group members.

Your GANG

Marshall Goldsmith once said, "Control your environment, or your environment will control you." We often think of our environment as the physical spaces and objects around us; however, we must consider another significant element: the people we surround ourselves with. Our thoughts shape our limits and what we believe is possible, and the people we choose to be around directly influence how we think and perceive limits and possibilities.

When you have the right GANG—a Goal-oriented Achieving Nudging

Group—you create a better environment for yourself and your GANG. Your GANG is a group of people with goals they want to achieve. I refer to a person's Mastermind Group, goal buddy, or accountability partner as their GANG.

Two key ingredients we often miss as we grow older and move forward are push and accountability.

Think of your GANG as a team. TEAM stands for: Together, Each Achieves More. From my personal experience, I work harder on a team, and I am more motivated when someone else is around. Having another person nearby helps me keep going when I am procrastinating. Your Mastermind Group is your GANG. It's your TEAM. They are the people you rely on for honest feedback, those you turn to when you are stuck and need that nudge. They are the people who know you well enough to call you out when you're lying to them or to yourself.

Your GANG will help you bring out your best, so you must be prepared to hear what you may not like or want to hear.

Self-employed Individuals need a GANG because when you're the boss, there is no one to hold you accountable. Ultimately, the customers do; however, it may be too late by then. It's all too easy to slough off, make excuses, and avoid being questioned. I admit, and often say, that for myself and probably for most others, we are our biggest obstacles and our biggest challenges. Aristotle said, *"The best victory is victory over self."*

It is just too easy to convince ourselves that whatever we're doing is the right thing, and there are reasons why we need to stay the same and not move forward. It is often fear, or sometimes it is the fact that we don't know what we don't know or refuse to see. It could be self-protection. Often left to our own devices and egos, we can get into trouble. We do not need "Yes" people because sometimes we do not see, refuse to see, or acknowledge a problem. Your GANG can help you open your eyes and confront what is holding you back.

It's easy to convince ourselves that what we're doing is right and that we should remain the same and avoid moving forward. Often, this mindset stems from fear or simply from not knowing what we don't know, or from refusing to face it.

Sometimes, it's about protecting ourselves. Left alone with our own egos, we can encounter trouble. We don't need people who simply say "Yes" all the time—because sometimes we miss or ignore problems.

Your team can help you see clearly and address what's holding you back.

Your GANG provides:

- Accountability
- Honesty
- Support
- Experiences of others
- Network

- A multitude of ideas
- Inspiration and motivation
- Clarity in goal-setting
- Encouragement

Mastermind Groups are Not Social Clubs

It's important to remember that this is not a social club; it is a Mastermind Group focused on your development and the development of others, emphasizing growth and success—whether in your business, personal life, or both. Usually, you don't achieve one without the other. The key is not to lose sight of the main objective of the group members: progress and growth.

While the group may engage in outside activities or fun events, it is crucial to maintain focus on the goal of long-term improvement. My group has hiked a couple of mountains and occasionally had dinner together; we even went bowling once.

However, it is worth repeating that keeping the focus on goals is essential. As you become closer and form friendships, it becomes much easier to overlook or ignore when a member is slacking, not completing their commitments, or not following the rules. It's natural for almost all of us to avoid conflict, which is the best reason to address issues early and nip them in the bud. This is vital for the health of the group.

Set up parameters for members to agree upon regarding calling out others for missing deadlines, targets, sloppy practices, and being unprepared for meetings. Always remember that this is about growth and development, nudging each other forward. When we catch issues early and make adjustments, it helps individuals who are falling short to grow. As an aside, these are times when an outside facilitator (which I will discuss later) can be beneficial. Accountability is what the group is about, and for many, both giving and receiving it can be challenging.

Accountability is an integral part of the process.

Another skill you will need to develop is diplomacy when working through group issues as they arise. One important thing to remember is that everything is easier if you "nip things in the bud." Periodically review your group's rules and individual commitments to keep them fresh in everyone's mind. Everyone should adhere to the group's rules, constantly reminding themselves that people can be sensitive and that others count on them.

I know I would have accomplished more, better, and faster with fewer mistakes if I had discovered the

UNLEASH THE POWER OF CONNECTION

Mastermind Principles and their power earlier in my life. They are an essential part of success for everyone, especially solo entrepreneurs, writers, speakers, and salespeople. Most of us know we can do better and that we need nudges. Another fact is that we always feel better when we have someone on our side, when we are part of a team and a group that supports us.

> *"Accountability is the sentry against Self-Sabotage. It doesn't limit us; it frees us to fly higher."*
>
> — Brendon Burchard

8

Under the Spotlight: Thriving in the Presence of Accountability

"Isolation is the enemy of excellence."

— Aaron Walker

Have you ever found yourself moving out of sight of a picture as if it were watching you? Even a picture can make us feel uncomfortable and watched, making us do better.

We Do Better When We Know Someone Is Watching

The following is from a 2020 article in the *Harvard Business Review by* Janina Steinmetz and Ayelet Fishbach:

- A powerful drain on your drive is a lack of other people watching you work.
- People are motivated to work harder when others are watching.
- People run faster, are more creative, and think harder about problems when observed.

The Hawthorne Effect

The Hawthorne Effect, credited to Elton Mayo, an Austrian psychologist, is the theory that people tend to work harder and more effectively for the team than for themselves. They may even be less inclined to give up or quit. Most of us will let ourselves down, yet we are unwilling to let the team down. This is part of our tribal nature; we are hyper-social beings. Social psychologists have long recognized that people tend to work harder when others are present or watching. People run faster, are more creative, and think more deeply about problems when they are observed or in a group. These effects occur for several reasons. People want to impress others through their performance and thus try harder—anyone who has ever stayed in the office late when their boss was still there has experienced this phenomenon.

Do you work harder on your own or when someone else is involved? A "team" doesn't have to mean a large group; sometimes, just one other person makes all the difference. When we're flying solo, it's all too easy to procrastinate or go easy on ourselves. But when you're part of a team, even a team of two, there's an energy shift. You feel more motivated, more accountable, and, oddly enough, work feels lighter. As John Donne once said, "Many hands make light work." I would say many hands help to push us and get things done.

Think about a time when you had someone supervising you or relying on you to complete a task. Sure, you may have felt a little pressure or nervousness, but that pressure often pushes us to rise to the occasion. It sharpens our focus, strengthens our resolve, and motivates us to take action. As I always say, it's a whole lot easier to let ourselves down than to let someone else down. That's why teaming up, even with one good partner, can be a wise choice for staying on track and getting more done.

A classic movie clip from the 1967 film *Cool Hand Luke*, titled *The Tar Sequence*, can be found on YouTube. In this pivotal scene, a group of prisoners, led by Luke, unites to outsmart their guards by completing their work ahead of schedule. They share a common goal and tackle the task with enthusiasm, finishing more than two hours early. They celebrate their victory over authority and ultimately find themselves with the rest of the day free from labor. This illustrates the power of a team.

Self-Awareness is Power

A Mastermind group is your team—whether it consists of an accountability partner, a goal buddy, or a small circle of trusted allies. For it to work, everyone needs a healthy dose of self-awareness and the honesty to share it. You need to know yourself: your motivation level, your strengths, your blind spots—and be willing to put that on the table. This prevents your team from wasting time second-guessing where you are or what kind of support you need. And let's be honest: we are much better at fooling ourselves than at fooling others. As Eric Hoffer wisely said, "We lie loudest when we lie to ourselves."

Let me give you an example. I would be better off developing my speaking, sales, or customer service skills than trying to become a computer programmer. Your primary goal should be to find what suits your personality, possibilities, and potential. You could even take tests like the Myers-Briggs, the Gallup StrengthsFinder, the Holland Code Career Test, and many others that may open your eyes and provide ideas about your possible direction.

You can set all the goals and attend all the seminars you want, but you still need an accountability system because, left to our own devices, we can mess up, get lazy, become distracted, or quit. Again, don't beat yourself up; it's called being human. We're all like that. Very few—and I mean very few—can thrive 100% or even 50% independently. It's part of being human, but it doesn't mean we should use our humanity as an excuse. We need accountability in all areas of our lives, including health, finances, work, and life goals, as well as in any other goal or project we want to accomplish.

Receiving high-quality feedback may not always feel like a valuable learning experience at the time; after all, we are human, and even the best of us can, at times, be vulnerable. If you genuinely want to grow, understand that tough feedback is a part of that growth. This is about personal development and success; as our parents have said, "It's for your good."

9

From Peer Support to Expert Guidance: Types of Mastermind Groups

Types of Mastermind Groups

"No two minds ever come together without creating a third, invisible, intangible force which may be likened to a third, invisible mind."

— Napoleon Hill

We tend to think of Mastermind Groups as business and personal development groups. However, there can be as many Mastermind Groups as there are occupations, hobbies, or industries. Some clubs, like Toastmasters, are excellent examples of less formal Mastermind Groups. Toastmasters helps people develop their public speaking and leadership skills; members receive mentorship and quality feedback, develop leadership abilities, and build confidence.

The primary purpose of a Mastermind Group is to learn, develop, share, and hold each other accountable. There is much less at stake in club-type groups than in personal development or business groups. Some groups require more accountability, while others are informal and relaxed. For example, a book club is a form of a Mastermind Group. These groups are more casual and may not need rules or may have very few, as seen in the book.

Who can form a Mastermind Group? Anyone! A Mastermind Group is an excellent choice for small business owners or entrepreneurs because they are often isolated while managing their day-to-day work; a group can serve as a board of directors. I have known many small business owners who have invited outside individuals to join their board of directors. They typically meet quarterly and have an agenda: the owner updates progress on goals, receives feedback and ideas, and is held accountable. It is easy for a business owner to become stuck without external accountability and connection with other business owners. When discussing Masterminds, we are referring more to working *on the business* versus working *in the business*.

The benefits of participating in Mastermind Groups include the variety of ideas, thoughts, and philosophies to which you might need exposure or have yet to consider. You gain many diverse ideas and experiences, so it is beneficial for your group to include people from different careers, businesses, and industries. One important aspect of a Mastermind Group is the diverse experiences of its members.

You or I would never live long enough to accumulate the collective experiences of everyone in the group. By being part of the group, you gain substantial input from many people's experiences, views, successes, failures, and lessons.

Mastermind groups can take various forms, ranging from more formal to less formal. However, they all share a common goal: to improve members' skills and work quality through information sharing and engagement.

Here are a few examples of the types of groups that could form a mastermind group:

Paid Groups: Paid mastermind groups are available, although I have never participated in one. In a paid group, members use their contributions to compensate the organizer, who controls and facilitates the group. These groups are beneficial because the facilitator is external to the group, keeps participants on track, and takes responsibility for the group's functioning and member commitment. It can be easy for individuals in a self-managed group to overlook issues, especially as the group coalesces and members become friends. Participants may overlook and allow others to slide when they are not fulfilling their commitments; this can negatively impact the group and potentially tarnish its reputation. This is also why rules and member commitments are important. More on this later.

Business Owners and entrepreneurs benefit from mastermind groups by gaining diverse perspectives and receiving support, accountability, and new ideas from their peers. These groups foster growth, problem-solving, and networking opportunities, enhancing leadership, decision-making, and business success.

Writers benefit from mastermind groups by receiving constructive feedback, encouragement, and a sense of accountability. They gain fresh perspectives, participate in brainstorming sessions, and access resources for overcoming challenges, which leads to improved writing skills, increased productivity, and a supportive community to navigate the creative journey.

Salespeople, such as those in my Top Guns sales mastermind group, benefit from sharing strategies, learning to overcome objections, and collaboratively refining sales techniques. They gain motivation, accountability, and insights from diverse experiences, resulting in enhanced skills, increased confidence, and improved sales performance.

A Quilting Group: A quilting group would benefit from a mastermind group by collectively sharing techniques, troubleshooting challenges, and inspiring creativity.

Toastmasters: Toastmasters provides public speaking skills, constructive feedback, and effective communication strategies.

Study Buddy: A study buddy increases accountability, effort, and grades.

These are just a few examples; as you can see, the possibilities for mastermind groups are endless. A mastermind group could help you improve anything you desire.

10

Annual Letter to Self

> *"If you don't know where you are going, you could end up someplace else."*
>
> —Yogi Berra, New York Yankees catcher and manager

The Letter to Self: Get Real, Get Clear, Get Going

The purpose of the *Letter to Self* is simple—but powerful. It serves as a reminder that you are capable, resourceful, and in charge of your own direction. It is a tool to help you get honest about what you want and what you *don't* want. Because let's face it: clarity isn't just about knowing your goals—it's also about eliminating distractions and dead ends.

Now, if this concept is new to you, don't worry. Most people don't make a habit of writing letters to themselves (unless they've time-traveled). It might feel strange at first—vulnerable, even. That's normal.

Getting real with yourself can feel like stepping into a spotlight you didn't ask for. But that's also where growth happens.

So here's the deal: this letter is for your eyes only—unless you choose to share it with your mastermind group. Think of it as a personal mission statement for the next 12 months. You will write down what you want to accomplish—concrete goals, not vague ideas—and the steps you are committed to taking. These can be bold leaps or small, strategic steps toward something bigger.

Either way, they matter.

This isn't fluff; it is a strategy and a compass. When done right, it becomes your yearly guidepost. If you share it with your accountability group, it transforms into a living tool for progress. They will help keep you on track, and you will do the same for them.

But here's the key: be brutally honest. Don't write what sounds good; write what *is* true. What do you really want? What are you actually willing to do? Imagine a no-nonsense drill sergeant standing next to you, barking, "Don't just talk. Commit. Follow through. No excuses."

The *Letter to Self* is about getting serious on your terms. So sit down, grab a pen, and step into your future with intention. You'll be amazed at what clarity—and a little pressure—can unlock.

UNLEASH THE POWER OF CONNECTION

> *"Make your plans ten times as great as you first planned; in twenty-five years from now, you will wonder why you didn't make them fifty times as great."*
>
> — Malcolm Forbes

Your Turn: Write Your Letter to Self

Take 20–30 minutes of quiet, uninterrupted time. This is your space to be honest, brave, and specific.

Prompt:

[Your Name] [Your Address]

[City, State, Zip Code] [Date]

Dear Future Me,

As I write this letter, I am filled with hope and determination for the year ahead. I want to take a moment to reflect on my goals and aspirations for the next 12 months.

1. Over the next year, I genuinely want to accomplish several key objectives. In terms of personal growth, I aim to read at least 12 books that challenge my perspectives and expand my knowledge.

In my business, I plan to launch a new product line that aligns with my values and meets the needs of my customers. I also want to strengthen my relationships by dedicating more quality time to my family and friends. Lastly, I am committed to improving my health by exercising regularly and adopting a balanced diet.

2. I am no longer willing to tolerate negativity in my life, whether it comes from external sources or my own self-doubt. I genuinely accept that I deserve to surround myself with positivity and support, and I will actively seek out environments that foster growth and encouragement.

3. To achieve these goals, I will take small but concrete steps. This month, I will create a reading list and set aside time each week to read. Next month, I will begin the research and development process for my new product line. This quarter, I will schedule weekly family dinners and commit to a workout routine that I can maintain.

4. I will reach out to my mastermind group and accountability partner for support. I will ask them to hold me accountable for my reading goals and to provide feedback on my product ideas. Their insights and encouragement will be invaluable as I navigate this journey.

5. This year, I will show up differently by embracing a mindset of growth and resilience. I will approach challenges with curiosity rather than fear, and I will practice gratitude daily. I will strive to be more present in my interactions, actively listening and engaging with those around me. I want to feel empowered and confident in my decisions, knowing that I am on the right path.

I look forward to reflecting on this letter a year from now and seeing how far I have come.

With determination,

[Your Name]

Reminder: This letter is *for your eyes only* (unless you choose to share it). Be real, be bold, and be kind to yourself—you're writing to someone who is doing their best.

When you're done, seal it in an envelope or save it in a digital folder labeled *Open in 12 Months*. Or, better yet, schedule a calendar reminder now.

You've got this.

Annual Letter to Self

During the following 12 months, I will accomplish the following:

1.
2.
3.

(Don't make the list too long. Remember, this is for the big stuff, not cleaning the garage.)

Sometimes, I've let myself down by setting goals (too large or too small), working toward them half-heartedly, or quitting. I am taking the following steps to minimize/reduce that risk.

1.
2.
3.

Starting today, I will develop a concrete plan to achieve my goals. I will create specific objectives with target dates and check-in points, and I will acknowledge possible roadblocks. I will check in with my group, goal buddy, or coach at least once a week.

This letter reminds me of what I am capable of and encourages me to establish a better path for myself. I want to use my abilities to become who and what I can truly be! Life is short; this is not a rehearsal.

Sincerely, You

Example

Annual Letter to Self

Over the next 12 months, I aim to achieve my health goal of losing 25 pounds.

(Don't make the list too long. Remember, this is for the big stuff, not cleaning the garage. You can even have addendums for each goal, but no more than two or three primary goals.)

Starting today, I am developing a concrete plan to achieve my goals. I will create specific objectives with target dates and checkpoints to ensure progress. I will designate time each week (or day) to work on my goals and devise a plan to overcome roadblocks and obstacles. I will check in with my group, goal buddy, or coach at least once a week.

Sometimes, I let myself down by setting goals and working toward them halfheartedly or quitting before I reach them. I am taking the following steps to improve my chances of success.

1. Report my progress to my Mastermind Group and accountability partner on a weekly basis.
2. Set specific times to work or go to the gym; the more detailed, the better. For example, I will go to the gym on Mondays, Thursdays, and Saturdays at 7:30 AM.
3. If I get lazy, I'll ask someone to remind me.
4. I will set myself up to succeed by making my mini-goals small and doable, thereby avoiding overload and failure.
5. If, for some reason, I miss, I will immediately start again.
6. I will hire a trainer.
7. Get help with my diet.

This letter reminds me of what I am capable of and to establish a better way for myself. I want to use my capabilities to be who and what I can truly be!

Sincerely, Your name

> *"No plan survives first contact with the enemy."*
>
> — Dwight D. Eisenhower

One of the maxims that many gurus tout in the success and positive thinking movement is, "You can accomplish anything; go for it, or just do it; you don't need a Plan B." This is horse manure, also known as BS; they rarely discuss obstacles as if they don't exist.

When people encounter barriers, they say to themselves, "Something is wrong; this isn't supposed to happen." Obstacles can feel like running into a brick wall. Yet, roadblocks, challenges, snags, SNAFUs, valleys, and complications will always be present. You know the saying, "Shit happens." Ignoring this fact can be detrimental to our goals. There will always be glitches, mistakes, and others who fall off or fail to deliver. Ignoring those possibilities and not planning for them is foolish.

It's essential to have a plan in place. If you need to improve your planning skills, ask for help. Stay mindful of potential obstacles from the start and throughout the process, and remember the Boy Scout and Girl Scout motto: "Be prepared." Be attentive, flexible, and willing to consider different options. While it's impossible to foresee every obstacle, try to anticipate challenges and plan how to overcome them as effectively as possible.

11

Finding Your Pace and Your A Team: The Key to Sustainable Success

Consistency is better than intensity

No One Goes 100%

If you listen to speakers on YouTube or at seminars, they often say things like, "Improve 1% every day for a year," and quote astronomical improvement numbers. Instinctively, we know this isn't true. I believe these kinds of statements can be more demotivating than motivating. We must remember that our brains have BS monitors. As I have said, no one is 100% all the time—not even the best of the best—so what about the rest of us? Setting big goals with small, sustainable steps helps you navigate the Valley of Dead Dreams, or at least makes it seem more like a small ravine. This is why having the right people in your corner is so important.

As for me and this book, I am nearing the end, so there is less to write. My goal of 400 words per day may be unsustainable and unnecessary. I have adjusted my daily goal to 200 words, which includes some editing and organizing. Trying to continue writing at the 400-word pace may lead to frustration, discouragement, a desire to give up, or the production of subpar work. It is better to adjust than to abandon a goal if you are still moving forward.

Pace

Have you ever noticed that when you're walking or running with someone, you tend to match their pace? What about that one slow driver who sets the pace and clogs up the highway? A driver going slower than the speed limit can back up traffic for miles or sometimes create a standstill. Remember, the same applies to your life and the company you keep.

The term "pace" has multiple meanings but generally refers to the speed or rate of progress. This concept can also be applied to your life. The people in your life play a significant role in determining your pace.

They are part of your environment and can either help you move forward or hold you back. It's important to ask yourself regularly who is setting the pace. Am I moving at the right pace? Am I slowing down or falling behind? This isn't about blaming; it is about taking charge, controlling your time and energy, and progressing toward your goals at a pace that works for you.

Answer these six questions:

1. What is the pace of my life?
2. Is this the pace I want?
3. Who is setting or influencing my pace?

UNLEASH THE POWER OF CONNECTION

4. How is it working for me at this moment?
5. How do I want it to work for me?
6. Do I need to make changes?

Remember: it's your life, your pace, your goals.

In his letters to Lucilius, the governor of Sicily, the Stoic philosopher Seneca wrote about his many friendships and said, "Associate with those who will make a better man of you. Welcome those whom you can improve."

Years ago, when I played racquetball, I competed against players of various skill levels. I was a solid B player. I never had formal coaching or lessons; I learned techniques through playing. I noticed that when I played with an "A" player, I had to elevate my game to match that person's level. Conversely, when I played against a C player, I rarely performed up to par. I occasionally lost to C players because I played down to their level rather than up to mine. This analogy applies to every aspect of your life. If you have C-level associations, you will perform at that level and lead a C-level life. Find your "A Team."

12

The Power of Goal Buddies, Coaches, and Mentors: Your Shortcut to Success

You won't go to the gym and attempt heavy bench presses without a "spotter." Why would you tackle the heavy lifting of your life—goals, dreams, and challenges—without one?

Mentors and coaches both support personal and professional development, but they differ in their approaches. A mentor is typically a more experienced individual who provides guidance based on their own experiences, focusing on the mentee's overall growth. In contrast, a coach is a professional who works with clients in a more formal relationship, helping them achieve specific goals and improve performance through a structured process.

> *"I use all the brains I have and all I can borrow."*
>
> — Woodrow Wilson, the 28th U.S. President

Those heading to the top always continue to receive coaching.

Coaches and Mentors Accountability

Most of us don't realize or think about all the coaches we have had. We've been coached by our parents, older siblings, teachers, athletic coaches, scouts, drama coaches, and even drill instructors, to name a few. Coaches surround our lives when we are young and tend to fade away as we age. One significant lesson is that people at the top of their game, or those heading to the top, always continue to receive coaching. We're talking about athletes, businesspeople, speakers, and the list goes on—basically, anyone who wants to improve and streamline their efforts.

Be mindful of the aspects of your life and career that could benefit from coaching and accountability. Understanding your strengths and weaknesses is essential, as is identifying areas where you may need motivation, support, or a push.

Individuals reading this book may have a business, want to start a business, have a sales career, write a book, or accomplish something else. From my experience, coaching is vital.

Suppose you are a business owner. When you're the boss, few people generally tell you when you're wrong or what you need to hear. This is not a good place to be; no one nudges you even when it's needed because you're the boss. If you fail to push yourself continually, you may experience periods of waxing and waning along your path.

Coaching will keep you moving forward. You may only need a little coaching—just a tune-up occasionally—

or you may opt for a weekly or monthly routine. It's all about what works for you.

Your coach focuses on helping you move forward. Even if you belong to a Mastermind Group, you may want a little extra one-on-one coaching. When you own a business, it's easy to put things aside and delay tasks that need to be done. Building accountability is essential.

Coaching is an ongoing process that keeps you focused and on the right track. A good coach will know when to nudge and support you. Coaching often requires an investment—think of it as a lifetime investment. Suppose you invest $5,000 into a coaching program, only to break even with a $5,000 increase in revenue that year (or whatever outcome you desire). Think of it as the beginning, for those results will compound year after year, just like money invested. It's the Compound Effect.

The Compound Effect influences everything. Everything in your business compounds; everything in your life compounds. In my book, *Suck It Up, Cupcake: Stop Screwing Yourself and Get the Life You Want,* I devoted an entire chapter to the "Compound Effect." It is so crucial that several books have been written on the power of compounding in life.

Coaching is like a large stone being dropped in a lake (your life); the waves ripple out in every direction, just like any positive or negative action ripples and permeates your life.

I hired a business coach, Mark, many years ago. Mark attended staff meetings every other week for over two years. We discussed goals and made plans, and he and I would meet in between. Mark was a very accomplished facilitator and implementer. He knew how to stay on track and keep you on track.

When we first talked about coaching, he reminded me, "I am not a good marketer." I replied, "I am, so we should complement each other," and we did.

I sent him 50% of his coaching business through my efforts for several years. What he did for me was help me get organized, stay on track, and hold everyone's feet to the fire, including my own. For over two years, we reorganized and updated the business. We worked towards setting ourselves up for our state association's Five Star program, which is equivalent to best practices for most companies. Then, it was time for the final interviews. Consultants reviewed the business model and all our processes, analyzing and evaluating everything, including the staff. We received the Five Star designation!

This is the power of having the right coaches and mentors. As an aside, this is why it is always valuable to know your strengths and weaknesses so that you can fill the gaps. Remember that no one has it all and can do it all; finding people who complement one another can make them unstoppable.

Eat a Banana

Years ago, I attended a workshop in Providence, Rhode Island, where the speaker, a very accomplished man, told us he had decided to run a marathon. He hired a trainer to help him. However, he began to experience leg cramps while running. Unsure of what to do, he told his coach, who suggested, "Eat a banana." Eat a banana? This high-powered professional speaker was uninterested in something as mundane and simple as "Eat a banana." He wanted some fancy, high-priced, jargon-filled, technical mumbo-jumbo about how to solve his problem. He thought he could buy a new magic elixir or potion to eliminate the cramping. Eating a banana was just too simple. However, he yielded to his coach's advice and ate a few bananas daily. Voila! The cramping eased and vanished in a few days. The coach knew all the technical mumbo-jumbo and understood why the bananas would work; that was all that mattered. Having a coach is like hitting a shortcut on your computer keyboard; it skips unnecessary steps.

Suppose you can't afford a coach; perhaps you're just getting started and don't have extra money to spare. If you have a coach or mentor who lives nearby, consider offering to exchange services with them.

For instance, you could mow their lawn, babysit their children, help them clean their garage, run errands, or assist with office work. You'll find that most people are willing to work with you.

Following through on your end of the bargain is crucial, which means putting in the work and practicing what you are learning from coaches and mentors. You can save time by listening, evaluating, and applying what they know, thereby avoiding the need to learn things the hard way.

I have had a few mentors in my life. The first was a successful man who owned a famous restaurant called Rom's Restaurant. It was once among the top 100 grossing single-location restaurants in the United States. Although I didn't know it at the time, he often gave me advice and mentored me. One thing he encouraged me to do was read—not novels, but books or journals that could help me advance. Eventually, I learned to appreciate reading and became an avid reader and learner.

The most valuable piece of advice Rom gave me was about business. He said, "Dennis, make sure that people always genuinely need whatever you are selling."

He explained that this is why he didn't sell fancy food at his restaurant. Instead, he provided his customers with value and filled their stomachs with good food. He believed that when tough times came, people would still come to his restaurant because they always needed to eat and appreciated the value it offered. His words inspired me to start my insurance agency, real estate company, and investment company. Rom was a business genius, always looking to develop new products and ideas to improve his restaurant. He was an avid reader, which significantly influenced his success.

Here is a classic example: In 1967, he came to me and said, "Dennis, more and more women are working extra hard and often away from home. They need a break sometimes. What we're going to do is take this special cardboard bucket, put 14 pieces of chicken in it, along with some pasta or French fries—whichever they prefer. We're going to give them some bread, some parmesan cheese, and salad, and we'll call it

Rom's Chicken in a Bucket." He was right. He sold what people needed and wanted, which was a massive success. Even today, people still talk about Rom's Chicken in a Bucket.

The best thing was that all that powerful advice was free; I just had to listen and, most importantly, take action.

I worked for just a little above minimum wage and received an education that set me on the path to wealth. As the credit card commercial says, "priceless."

My Coach Kenneth Crannell

At one point, I considered taking on more public speaking engagements and decided to take steps to improve. Through a friend at the National Speakers Association (NSA), I was introduced to Kenneth Crannell. Ken, a professor emeritus from Emerson College, was renowned for his innovation, talent, and tough demeanor. His students included famous media personalities such as Henry Winkler and Jay Leno.

When I mustered the courage to ask Ken about coaching, he requested that I send him a DVD of one of my speeches. He responded with a three-page letter detailing how I could improve but assured me that we could fix it. For several months, I made the trek to Saugus, Massachusetts, every three weeks for two- to three-hour sessions. Ken's coaching was transformative. He was an excellent but demanding coach, often apologizing for his tough approach. My response was always the same: "My father was an Army drill instructor; tough is not a problem."

Ken's coaching was the best I ever received. My only regret is not doing more. As Ken aged and his health declined, we transitioned to livestream coaching. The time, energy, and money I invested in Ken's coaching were invaluable. It felt like taking a giant step forward.

If you're considering coaching to improve any aspect of your life, do it. It's a significant investment that pays off for a lifetime. Although Ken passed away in 2016, his impact on my life and many others will be remembered for a long time.

Coaching will have a lifelong effect on you.

13

Finding Your Tribe: Selecting Members for Maximum Impact

Choose Members Wisely

Members need to relate to one another. Can you see yourself being friends or at least spending non-work time with the members of this group? You will likely spend at least a few hours with your Mastermind members each month. If you don't have similar commitments, the group won't work. It's better to find out sooner rather than later—a reminder: neither you nor others will be perfect. Members will make mistakes, waste time, and goof off. Do your best to keep everyone, including yourself, on track.

Another thing to consider is the mix of members coming right out of college and those who have years of experience. This may not work. Members should have some similar experiences; if not, there will be an imbalance in sharing, and the value gained may be lopsided. More experienced members may gradually drift away or begin to view the group as a mentoring session rather than a Mastermind Group.

Now that I have said that, let me somewhat contradict myself. A younger member may offer a fresh point of view and ideas, raise interesting questions, or have different methods. The group decides...

Avoid direct competitors. Providing objective feedback or recommendations to or from a direct competitor can be a challenging task.

Who Should <u>Not</u> Be Part of Your Group In my opinion:

- Your spouse/partner
- Direct competitors
- Employees
- Your boss
- People with no experience

New Members

If a situation arises, such as losing a member, you must decide whether to bring in a new member and what the process will be. One consideration is that if you have been meeting for some time, you have already created a certain level of intimacy and trust within the group, and introducing a new face may be unsettling. Doing this requires the utmost care and openness within the group before entertaining a candidate. There is also the risk that a member may advocate for someone whom the other members do not like or want. This is where having a clear consensus on the rules and procedures is essential. You don't want the wrong person or hurt feelings to affect the group. This may be a good reason to stick with whoever remains in the group.

What about a member who is falling off? How do you re-engage people who are falling behind? How do you encourage them? How do you get them to keep their commitments? You may not be able to do so. You may need to implement the "three strikes, and you're out" rule. It is up to the group; everyone needs to know the rules. It's important to review them often. The most important thing is to address these situations early.

"Most never run far enough on their first wind to find out they've got a second. Give your dreams all you've got, and you'll be amazed at the energy that comes out of you."

— William James

14

Meeting Structure Options

Meeting Structure and Options

Example of an Agenda:

Mastermind Meeting Agenda:

- 6:30-6:45 Open Chat (Optional, can always be before the official meeting)
- 6:45-7:00 Issues discussion & old business
- 7:00-7:45 Review the prior month and set new goals & actions (individuals come prepared with goals for the next month; also, acknowledging obstacles is a good idea)
- 7:45-8:00 Free discussion and close (or more goal-setting time)

Meetings can be longer than the duration mentioned above, but they usually won't be shorter unless it's a small group or just two people.

Some groups allocate two minutes for each member and then have a "Hot Seat," where one person, often for 15 minutes, presents their goals, actions, and obstacles since the last meeting, discusses whether they fell off course, and outlines what corrective actions will be taken. A member can also request additional time before a meeting. Asking beforehand is preferable because it is easier to manage, allowing the group to plan and adjust timetables in advance.

Obstacles

People often overlook potential obstacles and rush ahead without considering what could get in their way, whether those are external factors beyond their control or internal challenges. It's important not to deny or minimize these obstacles.

Maintain your focus on the goal. Achieving consensus at the beginning is crucial, and as time progresses, it is vital to keep members engaged in the process and structure.

Refreshments

Food may be part of the group meetings, depending on the time of day and location. As stated, restaurants can be distracting, and these distractions work against you.

The group I led for ten years started at 6:30 p.m. We had a potluck dinner, and everyone brought something. Often, one of the members would bring wine or beer, which is acceptable as long as the work gets done. Again, the group makes all the decisions.

The Longevity of the Group: Avoid Getting Stale

Groups can vary in duration. A key consideration is the group's value to its members. The length of time a group will function depends on several factors. For example:

1. Is everyone participating?
2. Are members getting what they need?
3. Are meetings getting stale?
4. Has it turned into a social time?
5. Are members showing up?

When you notice a disconnect, address it as soon as possible. People can become unfocused and disinterested, or the group can transform into something that is not functional. If group members have changed or if you have outgrown the group, consider leaving, adjusting, or disbanding it. This also applies to mentors, coaching, and goal buddies.

Leaving the Group

Earlier, I mentioned that people might leave the group for various reasons, such as family situations, illness, relocation, or career changes. Some may leave because they have not adapted to the pressure of performing, being accountable, or focusing on tasks until they are completed. Others may leave because the group no longer serves their needs. In the latter situation, it is best for them to leave sooner rather than later. It is a good idea to have a debriefing to discuss what the individual liked, what they found helpful, and what could be improved.

15

Commitment Devices (Bonus Chapter)

> *"You are always in a battle with your present self versus your future self."*
>
> — Daniel Goldstein

Commitment Devices — Building Unshakable Structures for Success

We all have goals and dreams—a vision of our future selves achieving meaningful and important things. Yet, to make that vision a reality, we must win the battle within. This is the fight between our long-term aspirations, represented by our future self, and our present desires for instant gratification, represented by our present self. All the tools presented in this book exist for one purpose: to help you win this battle. When you don't use tools like mastermind groups, accountability partners, or commitment devices (which we'll explore here), you miss out on powerful resources, effectively telling yourself, "I don't want to succeed." You're giving your present self permission to let your future self pay the price.

As I mentioned earlier, find what works best for you; often, it is beneficial to start small and allow your efforts to build. Brick by brick, tool by tool, you create a system in which your future thrives more often than it falters.

Something else to ponder: People tend to overestimate what they can accomplish in the short term and wildly underestimate what they can achieve over the long term.

It's not about intensity; it's about consistency. It is about your system(s) because consistency and sound systems always win. As James Clear said in his book *Atomic Habits,* "You do not rise to the level of your goals; you fall to the level of your systems."

Here is something else to ponder: people tend to overestimate what they can do in the short term and wildly underestimate what they can achieve over the long term.

What Are Commitment Devices?

Commitment devices are tools that help you stick to your intentions by modifying your behaviors and environment, thereby increasing or decreasing friction. Think of friction in the scientific sense: when there is more friction, movement slows down; when there is less, it speeds up. In life, the same idea applies. It's just like the brakes in a car. When you push the brake, you create more friction, which slows you down. When you release it, you speed up.

- **Increase friction** for behaviors you want to avoid.
- **Decrease friction** for behaviors you want to build.

For example, consider this old, trite but very true fact: if you're trying to eat less junk food, don't buy it — or if you do, store it in a locked cabinet across the house or in the back shed, where creatures will get you if you go out at night. This makes indulging more difficult, raising friction.

A friend of mine, Bob, ran a business and set up a second office a couple of miles from his main one. There were no phones and no distractions — just a desk, a chair, and internet access strictly for work. It was his fortress for deep, strategic thinking. By stripping the environment of everything nonessential, Bob reduced the friction around doing important work and locked himself into progress. That's a textbook commitment device in action.

Why Commitment Devices Work

Willpower fades. Motivation comes and goes, but structure *sticks*.

Commitment devices protect you on your worst days, not your best. They operate like a one-way door — you lock it behind you, so there's no going back. They don't necessarily make your goals easier; instead, they make *quitting* harder.

By purposefully creating friction for unhealthy choices and lowering friction for healthy ones, you stack the deck in your favor. In other words, you make doing the right thing the path of least resistance.

Here's the truth: sometimes the best way to help our future selves is to make certain decisions non-negotiable. Canceling temptations, locking away easy escapes, pre-paying for your gym membership, and sharing your goals publicly so others hold you accountable are all actions that establish a structure that endures when your willpower is running on empty, allowing you to retreat.

Build a structure so strong that your present self cannot sabotage your future self.

So, start today—no giant leaps, just small steps, one after another. Turn commitment devices into your allies. The future you will thank you. All you have to do right now is begin.

Examples of Commitment Devices: Scheduling

Setting aside specific times to complete important tasks—and creating the right environment with fewer distractions—will help you stay focused and follow through.

Accountability Partners

Meeting someone regularly to work, exercise, walk, or practice adds built-in accountability. You're more likely to show up when someone else is counting on you.

Personal Example

When I was in eighth grade, I committed to a fully scheduled study routine—something I had never done before. I stuck to it. The result? I had more free time, felt better about myself, and—for the first time in my life—made the honor roll.

Social Contracts

Sharing goals and progress with friends or family creates a support system and accountability.

(Be aware that some research has shown that when we tell others about our goals, it gives us a euphoric sensation, pumps up our dopamine, and sometimes can sabotage us because we feel like we've already accomplished something. This is based on scientific research.)

Mastermind Group, Accountability Partner

Human connection is the best, as long as you have an accountability partner or are part of a Mastermind group that will do their job. They are the commitment device of the highest order.

Behavior Contracts, with monetary penalties

A signed contract with your accountability partner for specific tasks or goals within a given time frame, usually best to do one month at a time.

Monetary Contracts

Pledging money to a cause you dislike if you fail to meet your goal creates a financial incentive.

Stickk.com and Accountability Contracts

Stickk.com is a popular online platform that brings accountability contracts to life. On the site, you set a specific goal and create a commitment contract—a binding agreement backed by your own money. If you fail to meet your goal, you forfeit your money, often donating it to a charity, an anti-charity, or even a friend (depending on how much you want the sting). Research shows that using Stickk's method makes you two to three times more likely to achieve your goals.

In the mastermind groups I've led, we used a similar approach. Members created commitment contracts with their accountability partners, complete with financial penalties for failing to follow through. The monetary consequence wasn't the point; it was the leverage, and it works.

You can download a sample contract at www.dennismccurdy.com

Public Declarations

Sharing goals openly and creating social pressure to follow through on them. (Again, beware, as mentioned in the Social Contracts section above.)

Technology-Based Tools

Using apps to track progress, set reminders, or block access to distractions.

Obstacles to Temptation

Limiting access to social media, putting your phone away, or using app blockers to restrict access to certain applications.

Physical Devices

A timer that vibrates to remind you to complete a task.

Limiting Access

Subscribing to services that provide healthy meal plans or educational content.

Automatic Paycheck Routing

Routing a portion of your paycheck automatically to your savings account makes saving easier.

A commitment account where withdrawals are limited helps individuals save more.

You know what's hard? Skipping the thing you *want now* for something you **might get later**. It's like watching everyone eat cake while you nod and say, "No thanks, I'm investing in my future self."

There are many ways to commit and take action; use what works best for you.

To conclude this bonus chapter, I will quote a few words from the book *As a Man Thinketh* by James Allen, published in 1903. Life is all about what we, as men and women, think. I read two pages of this book every single morning, and I mean every morning.

"The thoughtless, the ignorant, and the indolent, seeing only the apparent effects of things and not the things themselves, talk of luck, fortune, and chance. When they see a person grow rich, they say, 'How lucky they are!' Observing another become intellectual, they claim, 'How highly favored they are!' And noting the saintly character and wide influence of another, they remark, 'How chance favors them at every turn.'"

They do not see the trials in the failures and the struggles that these people have voluntarily encountered to gain their experience; they do not know the sacrifices they have made, the undaunted efforts they have put forth, and the faith they have exercised so that they might overcome the apparently insurmountable and realize the vision of their hearts. They do not know the darkness and the headaches; they only see the light and the joy, and they call it luck.

UNLEASH THE POWER OF CONNECTION

They do not see the long and arduous journey but only behold the pleasant goal and call that good fortune; they do not understand the process but only perceive the result and call it chance.

In all human affairs, there are efforts and there are results, and the strength of the effort is the measure of the result. Chance is not. Gifts, powers, and material, intellectual, and spiritual possessions are the fruits of effort; they are thoughts completed, objectives accomplished, and visions realized. The vision that you glorify in your mind, the ideal that you have growing in your heart—this you will build your life by; this you will become."

Find something short to read every day to keep you grounded in yourself and your goals.

Conclusion: Continue the Journey, Life Long Allies

Accountability: the word alone sounds like a chore chart for adults—but it's actually the secret sauce for growth, success, and, yes, happiness, as well as just about everything else. Whether it's your waistline, your wallet, your willpower, or your wild dreams, a little accountability goes a long way. Yes, holding yourself accountable can feel like voluntarily signing up for a root canal—but here's the twist: the results are glorious.

Nobody loves being dragged out of their comfort zone, but everybody loves fitting into their jeans, hitting financial goals, or finally finishing that project they've been working on for ten years. Accountability might not be fun, but neither is regret.

Choose wisely.

My experience with the Mastermind process and having an accountability partner or goal buddy has been truly enriching. It has pushed me to grow, and I've witnessed the same growth in others through Mastermind Groups or partnerships with accountability buddies, goal partners, or coaches. When I wasn't part of an accountability group, I didn't push myself as hard; it was too easy to make excuses. And trust me, we're all "Excuse Masters." It's easy to stay in our comfort zones or deceive ourselves. I believe in the power of accountability for everyone. The key is to find the approach that works best for you.

This process can truly make a difference in your life, and I'm confident it will help anyone who commits to it.

> *"At dawn, when you have trouble getting out of bed, tell yourself: "I have to go to work - as a human being. What do I have to complain of, if I'm going to do what I was born for - the things I was brought into the world to do? Or is this what I was created for: to huddle under the blankets and stay warm?"*
>
> *— Marcus Aurelius*

Mastermind is one of the best tools for pushing you to achieve.

- The masterminds, coaches, goal buddies, and accountability partners are magical.
  - They provide support, motivation, and guidance to help individuals achieve their goals and create positive change.
- We work harder when we know someone is watching.
- Holding someone accountable is a way to affirm and show that you care about their progress.
- Mastermind is not for everyone; it requires a strong commitment.
- Consistency is important.
- A good technique is to set achievable goals with a clear plan and to monitor progress through an annual letter to oneself.
- Avoid being caught in the thick of thin things.
- Keep things small. **KISSES**: **K**eep **I**t **S**imple, **S**ustainable, **E**asy, and **S**upported.

Reminders

- We are the average of the five people with whom we spend the most time.
- Be careful when selecting group members.
- Determine the time and day for meetings.
- Weekly meetings may be the most productive.
- Create a distraction-free environment.
- Allocate some time for casual conversation.

- Establish group standards.
- Have a clear structure for meetings.
- Establish accountability for meetings.
- Consider implementing penalties for persistent non-attendance.
- Share the highs and lows of the week.
- Designate one member to be in the "hot seat" at each meeting.
- Discuss the biggest goals and remember the small steps in between.
- Ensure that each member's plan and goals have detailed steps and clarity.
- Schedule additional in-between calls if needed.
- Use Commitment Derives to support work in a Mastermind Group.

"It is essential to have good tools, but it is also essential that the tools should be used in the right way."

— Wallace D. Wattle, Author, The Science of Getting Rich

If you cannot find a Mastermind Group, start one. You have the tools here; use them.

DENNIS A. McCURDY

The Mastermind concept is a proven process and a tool that will work for you if you take responsibility and do the work. Let the collaboration begin.

"You can't go back and change the beginning, but you can start where you are and change the ending."

— C.S. Lewis

The Beginning

UNLEASH THE POWER OF CONNECTION

Bulk Order Page

If you enjoyed this book, why not share it with friends, your team, or your group?

It can be a great stocking stuffer or thank-you gift.

10-20 books, $12.00 each plus shipping
21-50 books, $10.00 each plus shipping

For larger orders or additional information

Contact Dennis, 508-347-0810
mccurdydennis@gmail.com
Speaking, training, bulk orders, or questions

www.ingramcontent.com/pod-product-compliance
Lightning Source LLC
Chambersburg PA
CBHW062243300426
44110CB00034B/1569